SURPRISING SCIENCE

iPads

Ruth Beale

Cavendish Square

New York

Published in 2014 by Cavendish Square Publishing, LLC
303 Park Avenue South, Suite 1247, New York, NY 10010
Copyright © 2014 by Cavendish Square Publishing, LLC

First Edition

This publication represents the opinions and views of the author based on his or her personal experience, knowledge, and research. The information in this book serves as a general guide only. The author and publisher have used their best efforts in preparing this book and disclaim liability rising directly or indirectly from the use and application of this book.

CPSIA Compliance Information: Batch #WW14CSQ

All websites were available and accurate when this book was sent to press.

Library of Congress Cataloging-in-Publication Data
Beale, Ruth.
iPads / by Ruth Beale.
p. cm. — (Surprising science)
Includes index.
ISBN 978-1-62712-325-9 (hardcover)
ISBN 978-1-62712-326-6 (paperback)
ISBN 978-1-62712-327-3 (ebook)
1. iPad (Computer) — Juvenile literature. 2. Computers and children — Juvenile literature. I. Title.
QA76.8.I863 B43 2014
004.16—dc23

Printed in the United States of America

The photographs in this book are used by permission and through the courtesy of: Cover photo by © Mila Semenova/Shutterstock.com; © Mila Semenova/Shutterstock.com, 1; © Subbotina Anna/Shutterstock.com, 3; © Sergey Nivens/Shutterstock.com, 4, 8, 14, 18; © Quadrum solutions.pvt.ltd, 4; © Andy Dean Photography/Shutterstock.com, 5; Nzeemin/Newton Message Pad 120 stylus/own work/Creative Commons Attribution-Share Alike 3.0 Unported license, 6; © Jared C. Benedict/commons.wikimedia.org, 7; © Zach Vega/commons.wikimedia.org, 7; © Kyro/commons.wikimedia.org, 7 Ursprünglich von © Kyro, weiterverarbeitet von IWorld /commons.wikimedia.org, 7; Zach Vega, derivative work: Lolametro/ commons.wikimedia.org, 8; © David Orcea/Shutterstock.com, 9; © zach vega, commons.wikimedia.org, 9; © Quadrum solutions.pvt.ltd, 10; © Cheryl Casey/Shutterstock.com, 11; Matt Buchanan/Apple iPad Event03/originally posted to Flickr/Creative Commons Attribution 2.0 Generic License, 12; © maxhphoto/Shutterstock.com, 13; © zach vega, commons.wikimedia.org, 14; http://www.shutterstock.com/gallery-461077p1.html © Quadrum solutions.pvt.ltd , 14; © Quadrum solutions.pvt.ltd, 15; © 1000 Words/Shutterstock.com, 16; © zach vega, commons.wikimedia.org, 17; © Quadrum solutions.pvt.ltd, 17; © Denys Prykhodov/Shutterstock.com, 18; © Zach Vega, derivative work: Lolametro/ commons.wikimedia.org, 19; © Quadrum solutions.pvt.ltd, 20; © bloomua/Shutterstock.com, 21.

Editorial Director: Dean Miller
Art Director: Jeffrey Talbot

Content and Design by quadrum®
www.quadrumltd.com

iPads

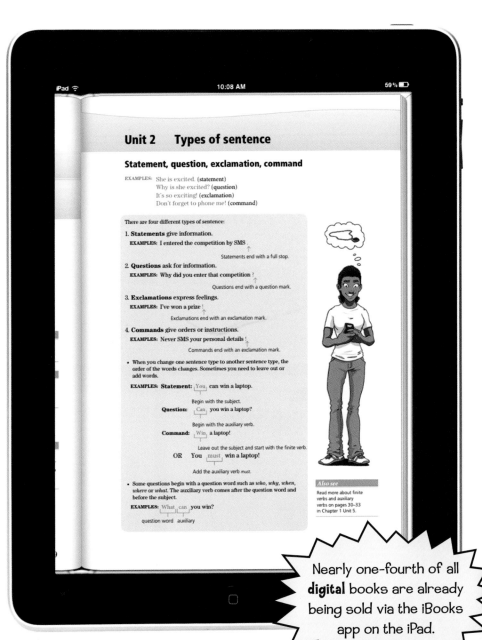

CHAPTER 1

Unit 2   Types of sentence

Statement, question, exclamation, command

EXAMPLES: She is excited. (**statement**)
Why is she excited? (**question**)
It's so exciting! (**exclamation**)
Don't forget to phone me! (**command**)

There are four different types of sentence:

1. **Statements** give information.

EXAMPLES: I entered the competition by SMS .

Statements end with a full stop.

2. **Questions** ask for information.

EXAMPLES: Why did you enter that competition ?

Questions end with a question mark.

3. **Exclamations** express feelings.

EXAMPLES: I've won a prize !

Exclamations end with an exclamation mark.

4. **Commands** give orders or instructions.

EXAMPLES: Never SMS your personal details !

Commands end with an exclamation mark.

- When you change one sentence type to another sentence type, the order of the words changes. Sometimes you need to leave out or add words.

EXAMPLES: **Statement:**   You can win a laptop.

Begin with the subject.

Question: Can you win a laptop?

Begin with the auxiliary verb.

Command: Win a laptop!

Leave out the subject and start with the finite verb.

OR   You must win a laptop!

Add the auxiliary verb *must*.

- Some questions begin with a question word such as *who, why, when, where* or *what*. The auxiliary verb comes after the question word and before the subject.

EXAMPLES: What can you win?

question word   auxiliary

Also see

Read more about finite verbs and auxiliary verbs on pages 30–33 in Chapter 1 Unit 5.

Nearly one-fourth of all **digital** books are already being sold via the iBooks app on the iPad.

Tale of the Tablet

Have you ever used an iPad? Isn't it interesting to read books and play games on it? Until just a few years ago, the iPad didn't even exist! No one read books on a computer; they simply picked a book up and browsed page after page.

An iPad is a recent **invention**. This **tablet** device was something many companies tried to make, but they just couldn't seem to get it right. Finally, after lots of thinking and creating, Apple came up with the iPad.

Newton

Names Dates Extras Undo Find Assist

6

Apple's first tablet computer was the Newton Message Pad 100, which was introduced in 1993.

Apple was already known for creating computers, iPods, and iPhones. On January 27, 2010, Steve Jobs, CEO of Apple Inc., stood in front of a roomful of people and announced his latest creation: a tablet-like device called the iPad.

Like all Apple products, the iPad's system and structure was hidden from the world. Before its release, journalists and bloggers were all wondering how the product would look and how it would work. No one would have to wait long—the first iPads were available in April 2010.

CHAPTER 2

The iPad has evolved a lot since its invention. There have already been five versions since its release!

How Does It Work?

The iPad works just like your normal computer, but its **compact** size and touch screen set it apart. The iPad runs on a super mini **micro processor** so you can carry it around easily. The smaller tablet also needs less power to run, so you can read, **browse**, and play for hours without having to charge your battery.

The fifth and latest version of the iPad is the iPad mini, which was released on November 2, 2012. It is smaller than a regular iPad, making it easier to carry around.

The new iPads have a higher resolution than most computer monitors and HD televisions! Better resolution makes your pictures and movies crystal clear—you can see all the colors and details.

The front of the iPad has a camera for Apple's "FaceTime" video chatting, while the back has a higher resolution camera for taking better photos.

Using your iPad (or any tablet) is easy because of its **touch-friendly interface**. You don't need a keyboard—you can touch things directly on the screen to launch apps, play games, or start and stop movies. Pinching two fingers together or apart lets you zoom in and out of pages and photos. You can even move things around to keep your iPad organized!

If you do need a keyboard to type something, it can appear right on the screen!

Applications on any tablet or smartphone are commonly called apps!

CHAPTER 3

One of the main reasons the iPad is so popular is because of its many apps!

Amazing Apps

If you own an iPad or any other tablet, you can do so much with it! You can start by using the built-in apps or ask your parents to get more apps for you from the App Store. You can read books, play games, watch movies, connect to the **Internet**, and do so much more!

Some apps are free but not all. Many free apps, such as Angry Bird and Temple Run, have become extremely popular. You should always ask your parents before downloading a new app.

There are iPad apps for almost anything you want to do. You can get apps for music, movies, magazines, news, games, and ebooks. There are also many educational apps. You can learn about any topic with apps that combine audio, video, animation, and illustration.

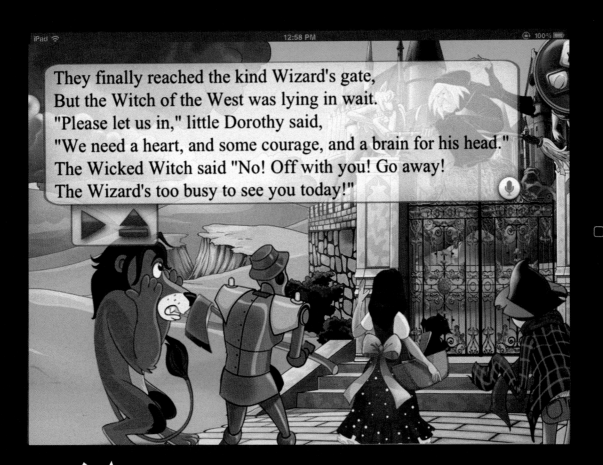

Ebooks are electronic books that are published in a digital format.

iCloud saves your information, movies, songs, and more in a special location. If you accidentally lose any of them, you can always get them back for your computer, iPad, iPhone, or iPod.

One of a Kind

The iPad comes with lots of applications built specifically for it. Apple even has its own operating system called iOS. It makes your iPad and apps run smoothly.

Some of the apps you will use often are the Web browser, Safari; the music and video store, iTunes; and the magazine and book application, Newsstand. Every day, people create new apps to help you do everything from watching a movie to studying school subjects!

Your iPad or any other tablet can download apps from your app store. The store is filled with awesome applications sorted into different categories. As soon as you choose a new app with your parent's permission, it instantly downloads to your tablet.

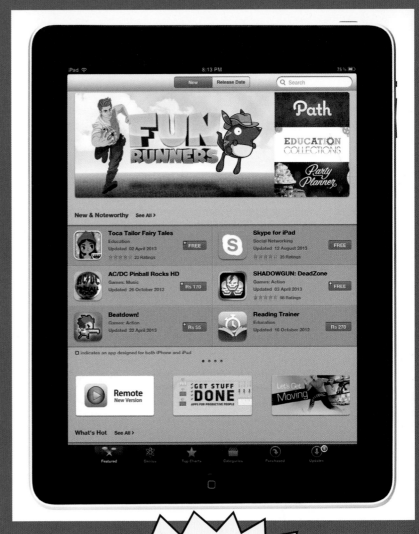

The Apple app store has about 500,000 apps, of which 65,000 are exclusively for the iPad!

Many applications, mainly games, make use of the iPad's **hardware** in various ways. These games can be controlled by rotating and tilting the device or enabling its **motion sensors**, while others rely on touch controls like tapping and swiping.

iPads also have a gyroscope, which rotates the screen for you! It is an accurate motion and tilt sensor that allows you to play games by tilting your iPad around. When you play a racing game and tilt your iPad to the right, the gyroscope makes your car turn right. That's how you can stay on the track and win the race!

Glossary

applications [app-li-KAY-shuns] computer software that helps the user perform multiple tasks

browse [BROWZ] look through data or sites on the Internet

compact [KOM-pakt] closely packed to reduce the size of something

digital [DIJ-ih-tal] a term relating to the usage of computers or electronics

hardware [HARD-ware] the mechanical, wiring, and other physical components of an electronic device

interface [IN-ter-face] the point of connection between a device's software or hardware

internet [IN-ter-net] a huge system of networks that links together information from all over the world

invention [in-VEN-shun] a unique and new creation

motion sensor [MO-shun SEN-sur] a device that detects moving objects

tablet [TAB-lit] a computer that is operated by touching the screen

touch friendly [TUCH FREND-lee] a device that can be controlled by the touch of a finger

Books to Discover

Cogert, Mitchell. *101 Top iPad Apps for Kids*. Scotts Valley, CA: Create Space, 2012.

Costello, Sam. *My iPad for Kids*. Boston: Pearson Education, 2012.

Proffitt, Brian. *iPad for Kids*. Boston: Course Technology, 2012.

Websites to Explore

iPads for Kids
http://www.ipad4kids.com/

How Stuff Works
http://www.howstuffworks.com/gadgets/high-tech-gadgets/ipad.htm

Amazing Apple Applications
http://www.apple.com/education/apps/

Index